Heaven in a Wild Flower

Joan Winmill Brown

Illustrated by Barbara Wilson

The C. R. Gibson Company
Norwalk, CT 06856

Published by The C. R. Gibson Company, Norwalk,
CT 06856

Printed in the U.S.A.

ISBN 0-8378-1841-9

GB 722

To my friend Ruth Graham who has so often shared with me the joy of the One who has made "all things bright and beautiful."

The idea for this book arose from a visit to Israel. It was springtime and masses of wild flowers were in bloom. The mountains, hills and valleys were awash with color—the reds, yellows, blues of the flowers that abound in the area. During my visit, there was a national alert—once more Israel faced invasion, but the wild flowers seemed to be a symbol of hope. Their tenacity and beauty were a testimony of God's faithfulness.

The history of the Holy Land has been a troubled one. One of invasion, war, devastation, famine, drought, pestilence. Still, the flowers faithfully burst into bloom each spring, seemingly unaware of their hostile surroundings. They comfort me when I think of their determination to bloom against all odds. Up through the arid soil, with a singleness of purpose, they fight their way into the sunlight to become beautiful and triumphant. Again, at precisely the right moment, God has made everything beautiful.

Flowers are often mentioned in the Bible. There are four that are special to me. The mustard flower is my symbol of faith; the rose of Sharon gives me the assurance of God's love; the anemone, called the "lily of the field", deepens my reality of His peace; and, finally, the heavenly blue flax flower brings me the joy of our Lord's promise of eternal life.

Each of these special flowers and the characteristic that I associate with it has memories for me, personal thoughts and experiences and those that others have shared with me. These memories bring me comfort and the assurance that God is with me in every experience of my life.

I hope that you, too, will enjoy them.

He has made everything
beautiful in its time…
Ecclesiastes 3:11

Mustard

faith

The mustard plant grows profusely throughout Israel. In spring, bright yellow flowers cluster upon each stem, making a vivid carpet of color across the great plain. The plants grow very tall, often obscuring a horse and rider from view. Birds are attracted to the flowers; finches and linnets dart among the plants. Jesus compared the mystery of the kingdom of heaven to a grain of mustard…

> "…which a man took and planted in his field. Though it is the smallest of all your seeds, yet when it grows, it is the largest of garden plants and becomes a tree, so that the birds of the air come and perch in its branches."

Matthew 13:31-32

Thoughts of mustard go back to my early childhood in England. I was often asked by my grandmother to make a stunningly-hot sauce for the roast beef by adding a little water to mustard powder and stirring until it was smooth. Grandmother would quote Matthew as we worked. "…If you have faith as small as a mustard seed, you can say to this mountain, 'Move from here to there' and it will move. Nothing will be impossible for you." Imagine that little girl sitting at the kitchen table, dreaming of being able to rearrange mountains…

Several years ago, as I walked along a dusty path outside the city walls of Jerusalem, I saw the mustard plant for the first time. I was amazed by its size.

The guide who was taking me to the Garden of Gethsemane stopped and picked a mustard flower and gave me some of the seeds. How small they were! If these tiny seeds could blossom into such large plants, could I not nurture a simple faith until it also grew…?

"Faith is a living and unshakable confidence,
a belief in the grace of God."

Martin Luther

In everything we do there is faith. I am English and four o'clock tea is a daily event. Unquestioningly, I turn on the faucet and expect water to fill my kettle. When I turn on the stove, I expect heat…

The gardener, too, experiences a similar faith—that a flower seed will germinate, that at the correct time a green shoot will herald a beautiful flower.

Yet, when a situation arises that seems to have no solution, we sometimes find it difficult to believe that God, who created the extraordinary beauty of this earth, is there. And, that in His time He will make something beautiful from the chaos.

Ella Wheeler Wilcox's inspiring poem "Faith" speaks to us of the undaunted spirit that comes when we learn to trust in God.

> I will not doubt, though all my ships at sea
> Come drifting home with broken masts and sails;
> I shall believe the Hand which never fails,
> From seeming evil worketh good to me;
> And, though I weep because those sails are
> battered,
> Still will I cry, while my best hopes lie,
> shattered,
> "I will trust in Thee."
>
> I will not doubt, though all my prayers return
> Unanswered from the still, white realm above;
> I shall believe it is an all-wise Love
> Which has refused those things for which I yearn;
> And though, at times, I cannot keep from grieving,
> Yet the pure ardor of my fixed believing
> Undimmed shall burn…

I remember a true story that a friend told me about a young couple and their children. The husband was a missionary and they were being sent to a remote part of Africa. There would be periods of separation as the husband traveled to other parts of the country. They accepted this as part of his work for the Lord, but, still, the wife dreaded the first separation in a foreign land. When it came, her husband had been gone for only a short time when one of her children contracted polio. There was no way to reach her husband. Night and day she stayed up to nurse her sick child and take care of their other little ones. After a month, her husband returned. The crisis was over. He had not even been aware that his child was gravely ill. As my friend listened to the wife tell this story, she said, "It must have been difficult for you. You must have prayed and prayed."

"Actually," the young mother answered, "I was so tired I could not even pray. But God gave me a sentence that I repeated over and over…*For this I have Jesus.* It was this knowledge that gave me strength to go on."

In every circumstance we face, even if we only have faith as small as a mustard seed, we can know that we have the presence and comfort of our Lord. In that young woman's simple, trusting words lies the key to serenity.

Trust in the Lord with all your heart
and lean not on your own
understanding;
in all your ways acknowledge him,
and he will make your paths
straight.

Proverbs 3:5-6

A dictionary defines faith as unquestioning belief, complete trust and confidence. But sometimes it is hard to trust—to wait for God to act in our lives. His timing often seems uncaring. We want answers immediately. When I first gave my life to Jesus Christ, there were instant answers to my prayers. I had no doubts. I trusted Him completely. It was weeks before I experienced my first feelings of unbelief. God had not chosen to answer a prayer of mine, and depression set in.

As I sat staring out of my window, things looked terribly bleak. Was my experience of simply trusting in a loving Father, who had sent His son to die for me, to be of no avail? I reached for my Bible and idly scanned the pages. Yes, I believed. But I had doubts. Then, I came across the account of the man who had come to Jesus, asking Him to heal his child...

"Everything is possible for him who believes."
Immediately the boy's father exclaimed, "I
do believe; help me overcome my unbelief!"

Mark 9:23-24

The honesty of that father's words gave me hope. Even in Jesus' presence he had doubts—but he acknowledged them, and asked for Jesus' help. I realized my feelings of unbelief were not unique. I got down on my knees and thanked our Lord for the reassuring words that I had read. Reading on, I saw that Jesus did heal the man's child. I knew that in time, God would answer my prayers, in His way. That day I learned that the greatest experience of communion with God comes when we truthfully pray from a completely trusting heart.

Mr. George Muller, a man of great faith, lived in the England of Charles Dickens, a time of great poverty. The living conditions of the poor were appalling. Muller was especially distressed by the great numbers of uncared-for orphans.

Muller's resources consisted of two shillings (about fifty cents) when God bade him start an orphanage. His faith inspired others to give—some women gave jewelry, others treasured heirlooms. Gifts of money would come from people who could barely afford them. All received inspiration from Muller's love for the children.

Often, funds would run out. One day, as the children assembled to eat, Muller knew that there was absolutely nothing to give them. The kitchen was bare. He prayed, believing, unquestioningly, that his prayers would be answered. The hungry children sat restlessly in the dining hall as he prayed.

A short time later a van pulled up to the door of the orphanage. The van was filled with bread. The owner of the bakery said that he had felt "compelled to send the bread."

"Give us this day our daily bread," was a prayer that George Muller believed, unwaveringly. For sixty years, this man of great faith fed and clothed thousands of children. Here in his own words, we see the secret of his unselfish success.

"Just in proportion to which we believe that God will do what He has said, so is our faith strong or weak. Faith has nothing to do with feelings, or with impressions, with improbabilities, or with outward appearances. If we desire to couple them with faith, then we are no longer resting on the word of God because faith needs nothing of the kind. Faith rests on the naked word of God. When we take Him at His word, the heart is at peace."

I remember a story about a little boy who lived near New York City, many years ago. It was Holy Week and the boy knew that his church would be conducting services each morning with a visiting minister in charge. On the Thursday morning before Easter, the boy awoke to the sound of rain on the roof. His first impulse was to stay in his warm bed. But he remembered the service and the visiting minister. Reluctantly, he got out of bed, dressed and made his way through the pouring rain to the little church.

He saw that he was the first to arrive. Dripping, he walked down the aisle and took a seat. The minister, a man with a bright red beard, greeted him, and, to the boy's surprise, began the service. The boy looked around, but there was no one else there. Hastily, he found his place in the prayer book and gave the appropriate responses. When it was time for the offering, the minister leaned forward with the plate and a wet coin was forthcoming. As the minister dedicated the offering, he touched the boy's head with his hand. Then, the sermon was preached to one small child, sitting in the front pew.

The faithfulness of the minister on that wet and dismal morning stayed with the little boy. Often he would remember the man's hand upon his head. The boy did not enter the ministry when he grew up, but he did serve God in a different way.

The boy's name was Cecil B. DeMille who would, one day, create "The King of Kings" and "The Ten Commandments," films that would make the Bible real to millions of people.

Rose of Sharon

love

Some botanists and Biblical scholars feel that the "rose" of Sharon is really a tulip. It still grows in abundance on the plain of Sharon, which stretches for sixty miles between Carmel and Jaffa. The traveler crossing this plain has a spectacular view. To the west, the sparkling blue Mediterranean and to the east, the great hills of Judah rising to meet the horizon. Much of the land is under cultivation, but where it is not, the rose of Sharon can be seen growing. The plant is about ten inches tall and the gray-green leaves contrast with the scarlet blossoms.

The word "love" is used often in the Bible. Indeed, love is basic to Christianity. God, our Heavenly Father, loves us unconditionally, unceasingly. It is difficult for our finite minds to imagine the immensity of His love. But, in Jesus, we are able to see God's love in action. The "Song of Solomon" is a celebration of the love between Jesus and His Church. King Solomon referred to Him as "the rose of Sharon and the lily of the fields", further reinforcing the association between love and the rose of Sharon.

O_n the road between Carmel and Jaffa, I saw the light spring breeze create a rippling effect across the great plain, where roses of Sharon bent and swayed in the wind, their strong, supple stems not resisting, but bending resiliently. Then the breeze stopped and the flowers righted themselves. They made me think of how important it is that we remain pliable in our spiritual lives. Not resisting God's will, but bending to His direction, obeying and ultimately becoming stronger and more joyous in our walk with Him.

> *...I delight in your commandments*
> *because I love them.*

Psalm 119:47

It is not always easy to bend; and, people often want us to. Immediately our antennae go up. We balk, dig in our heels and say, "NO!" How different it is when someone who loves us asks us to do something, someone we really love and respect. Then it is easy for us to surrender our own desires. The more we love God, through Jesus Christ, the easier it is to obey His commandments, for we know that He wants the very best for us.

W_{hen} Jesus traveled, He encountered people who lacked love in their lives and he was drawn to these needy people. The Bible tells us countless stories of Jesus' love. At the Pool of Bethesda, known for the healing quality of its water, He met a man who had waited 38 long years to be healed. On another occasion, among a crowd of followers, Jesus realized that he had been touched by a woman who longed to be made well. "Daughter, your faith has healed you..." Perhaps the most needy of all was the woman who walked among the mourners in a funeral procession coming out of the gates of Nain. This distraught woman had lost her son and now she was alone in the world.

When the Lord saw her, his heart went out
to her and he said, "Don't cry."

Luke 7:13

Then Jesus touched the body of her son and said, "Young man, I say unto thee, Arise." The boy sat up and began to speak. And Jesus, with great tenderness and love, "delivered him to his mother."

The tender love of Jesus Christ, the rose of Sharon, is with us each moment of our lives. You may feel as if you are only a face in the crowd, and that no one really knows how deeply you are hurting, but His love surrounds you and will never let you go.

I look to Thee in every need,
And never look in vain;
I feel Thy touch, Eternal Love
And all is well again....

Henry Wadsworth Longfellow

Jesus said, "As the Father loved Me, so love I you." It was this love that led Him to the Cross, and in that sacrificial act He set a precedent for all of us. There is nothing that we can do to measure up to such love, but by surrendering our hearts and wills to Him, we can begin to learn to love as He does.

When we know we are loved by God, we are able to face the future with assurance. We are able to reach out in Jesus' name to others in need.

One of the greatest examples of this is found in the dedicated life of Mother Teresa. This amazing woman came from a wealthy family, but when she responded to the call of God to care for the terminally ill, she willingly accepted a vow of poverty. Mother Teresa's total commitment has given the whole world a benevolent code by which to measure love and caring.

I shall never forget seeing this seemingly frail woman, dressed in a simple white sari, address the United Nations. Without fear or pretence, she spoke quietly, but with great authority, to the representatives of millions of people around the world. She spoke of God's love, ending with the simple, humble words of Saint Francis:

> *Lord, make me an instrument of Your peace.*
> *Where there is hatred, let me sow love;*
> *Where there is injury, pardon;*
> *Where there is doubt, faith;*
> *Where there is despair, hope;*
> *Where there is darkness, light;*
> *And where there is sadness, joy.*
>
> *O Divine Master, grant that I may not*
> *So much seek to be consoled as to console;*
> *To be understood as to understand;*
> *To be loved as to love;*
> *For it is in giving that we receive;*
> *It is in pardoning that we are pardoned;*
> *And it is in dying*
> *That we are born to eternal life.*

As she finished, men and women, some affluent, others from poor nations, rose to their feet and gave her a resounding, yet reverent, ovation. This indomitable woman was the epitome of Saint Francis' prayer. Her secret? Surely a completely surrendered life, and a close, loving walk each day with our Lord.

God may not call us to a life of poverty, working among the needy; all He asks is that we willingly surrender our lives to the "Rose of Sharon", so that we, too, may be able to show His love to those who need Him in the world around us.

Love of God makes us kind and compassionate. Mother Teresa exemplifies kindness and compassion for God's needy children. We can also see kindness and compassion of a great man for a poor orphan girl in this true story.

Around 1850, in an out-of-the-way town in Germany, a talented young orphan girl decided to give a piano recital. She was very poor and felt she could earn money this way. She went around the town putting up handmade posters that claimed she was a pupil of the famous Hungarian pianist and composer Franz Liszt. This was untrue, but she thought that it would draw a bigger audience.

All was going well until she learned, the day before her recital, that Liszt was in town. It was too late to take down the posters, and she was afraid that he would see them. After a great deal of soul searching, she realized there was only one thing to do—see him and explain why she had capitalized on his name.

The girl was granted an interview and during it she broke down and cried, telling Liszt what she had done, and asking his forgiveness.

The great musician listened quietly to her story, then said, "It was wrong for you to have told this lie, but all of us make mistakes. At these times there is only one thing we can do, and that is to be really sorry. I believe that you are. Now, let me hear you play."

Relieved, yet frightened, she began to play. She made many mistakes at first, but gradually her confidence took hold and she played well.

After listening to her, Liszt realized that she was an accomplished pianist, but he took the time to correct some of her phrasing. "Now, my dear, I have instructed you. You can say that you are a pupil of mine. You can give your recital. But, the final piece will be played by the master." Needless to say, the recital was a resounding success.

To those who fall, how kind thou art;
How good to those who seek;
But what to those who find? Ah, this
Not tongue nor pen can show:
The love of Jesus, what it is,
None but His loved ones know.

Bernard of Clairvaux

On a recent visit to London, a friend of mine told me a story that took place in one of the most luxurious hotels in the city.

The main character is an old Scotsman, whom I will call Mac. This man, who does odd jobs for my friend, sleeps in the parks of London. As she says, he sleeps "rough." One night, he was very hungry and decided to venture through the revolving door of a prestigious hotel in search of food. Somehow Mac, dressed in shabby clothes and none too clean, managed to evade the eagle eye of the hotel detectives and walked over to the main staircase.

Standing at the top was an elegantly-dressed woman—diamonds glittering—her formal evening gown of satin shimmering in the light. She was greeting her dinner guests. Mac hesitated for a moment, then walked up the stairs, and announced quite simply, "I'm hungry."

As this story was being related to me, I could not help but think of Jesus' parable of the rich man who was so angered when his guests did not arrive for dinner, that he told his servants to go out and bring in the poor and hungry to eat at his table. Here, the poor was coming, uninvited, to the dinner party.

The normal reaction might have been to call for the detective and have this shabbily-dressed old man escorted out. But, quite unruffled, and seeing the man's obvious need, the hostess ordered a place be laid for him. He sat with her guests, to their astonishment, and to the astonishment of the hotel staff.

After Mac had finished eating, he rose to leave. The woman's husband came up and shook him by the hand. Concealed in his palm were several pound notes. The other guests did not see this act of kindness, as the host wished Mac "God speed." I was reminded of Jesus' admonition that when we give not to let the left hand know what the right hand is doing.

As Mac thanked his host and hostess, and bade farewell to his fellow guests, the chef came out of the kitchen with a large parcel of food and gave this to him with a smile. Old Mac left the hotel, warmed not only by the food in his stomach, but by the generous and loving acts he had encountered.

I was very moved as I listened to my friend tell this story. This was love in action. It was like Jesus' love, there was no condescension, no display. Mac was treated with dignity. These people saw a man who was in need and responded with their hearts.

Jesus sees us as we are and loves us. He does not despise us if we are uneducated, or ill-clothed. He sees beyond the outer apparel, even if we are wearing designer-label clothes, and His love reaches down deep into our hearts. It is there that He meets our needs.

*Accept one another, then, just as
Christ accepted you, in order to
bring praise to God.*

Romans 15:7

Love has a hem to her garment
That trails in the very dust;
It can reach the stains of the streets and lanes,
And because it can, it must.

Author unknown

Lord, Your love reaches out to all who need You:
seeing beauty in a life others may have passed by—
"He's not worth trying to help—we've tried before."
We see people all around us who need Your
forgiving, forgetting the past love. The love that
can restore, make new again. The love that can break
the chains of habit that have helped destroy their
self-esteem. The love that can stop the treadmill
of failure after failure and change a despairing
life into one filled with hope. Not just for today, but
forever.

Teach us more of Your love, Lord, so that we can
reach out in Your name and tell a lonely, searching
heart that You came so that each one of us can bring
our lives to You. Piece by piece You lovingly restore
them—making them beautiful in Your time.

Anemone

peace

What are the "lilies of the field" so often mentioned in the Bible? Experts believe that this is a collective term used for some of the many wild flowers that grow in Israel. Although the narcissus, the chrysanthemum and the daisy are contenders for being included in this category, it is the crown anemone that is believed to reign as the "lily of the field."

Hundred of seedlets are formed every year in each flower and blown by the wind—the anemone is also called the windflower—and in early spring many thousands of these flowers burst into bloom. The majority are scarlet, but others are purple, pink, blue and white, making a magnificent splash of color upon the land. It is a favorite flower of spring.

When Jesus spoke words of peace and comfort to the multitudes near the plain of Gennesaret, an area known for its masses of flowers, he must have looked out over the anemones' brilliance, as he said:

"Therefore I tell you, do not worry about your life, what you will eat or drink; or about your body, what you will wear. Is not life more important than food, and the body more important than clothes?

...See how the lilies of the field grow. They do not labor or spin. Yet I tell you that not even Solomon in all his splendor was dressed like one of these.

Matthew 6:25,28-29

Imagine the resplendent, colored robes that King Solomon must have worn: the fine, vibrant silks of purple and scarlet—the magnificent gold crown that adorned his head. Such majestic splendor! Yet, Jesus said all that was nothing compared to the brilliant carpet of flowers that grew close to His feet as He spoke to the attentive crowd.

Forever beleaguered and badgered by the Roman invaders, the lives of these people were not their own; most merely existed. And then Jesus came into their midst and brought a message of hope and peace that anyone of them could experience.

It was natural for the people in the crowd to be concerned about where their food and clothing would come from, but Jesus said they should be anxious for nothing:

> *For the pagans run after all these things, and your heavenly Father knows that you need them. But seek first his kingdom and his righteousness, and all these things will be given to you as well.*
>
> Matthew 6:32-33

Fears can be paralyzing. Imagined fears about the future drain us of strength and creativity, and we cease to live the way God intended us to live.

King Alexander the Great was famous for his leadership in battle and his enemies feared him greatly. He was also known to have a special love and understanding of horses. He once saw a friend experiencing great difficulty controlling his mount; the animal was rearing and kicking, and was very frightened.

"Turn its head to the sun!" shouted the king.

With great difficulty, his friend was able to do so and, instantly, the horse became calm and manageable.

"It was frightened by its own prancing shadow," Alexander explained.

How many times are we frightened by the shadows in our own lives? The shadows of our fears. The fear of losing someone we love, the fear of illness, the fear of the future. But when we turn toward our Lord, the Son of God, we become calm in the light of His peace and love.

You will keep in perfect peace
him whose mind is steadfast,
because he trusts in you.

Isaiah 26:3

The Field of the Shepherds is situated about five miles outside of Bethlehem. Rolling hills form an impressive backdrop for the black Bedouin tents that dot the landscape. In the spring, the field is a mass of wildflowers.

It was here that David watched his father's flock and protected them from animals that preyed on the defenseless sheep. It was here that the angel appeared to the shepherds to tell them that there was no need to be afraid of the heavenly apparition. In the distance, a bright star shone over the town of Bethlehem, directing their way to the stable where Jesus was born that night. "…a Savior, which is Christ the Lord…"

A few years ago, I walked in that same field and turned to look back at the city of Bethlehem, the city that would always be remembered as the place of Jesus' birth. I imagined what it must have been like for the shepherds as they walked toward that city. They must have been fearful, yet filled with great anticipation. The Messiah who had been promised for so many years was finally here! His coming promised a peace that would remain deep within the soul of all who accepted Him.

Peace I leave with you; my peace I give you. I do not give to you as the world gives. Do not let your hearts be troubled and do not be afraid.

John 14:27

We often fail to remember God's watchful care. Caught up in tensions, we forget to reach out to Him for His unfailing help. I wrote the following prayer after a day when I had tried to do everything in my own strength, and had failed miserably.

*I cannot find peace in this swirling, stressful
day, Lord. Everything comes in on me like
a great cacophony of sound, and all that You
taught me in the quiet moments is somehow
forgotten. My troubled mind is filled with the
echoes of regrets and discordant memories. I
have failed to love as I should—live as I should.*

*Yet, in the midst of all these thoughts, Lord, I am
reminded of a field—the Field of the Shepherds—
where I once walked and saw the scarlet anemones
growing, their faces upturned to the sun.
"They toil not, neither do they spin…"
Your words come back to me: stopping my
turbulent thoughts, making me realize
that once more I am toiling, not trusting
You for peace—for strength.*

*Forgive me, Lord, and teach me more of Your
infinite peace that can completely embrace my frail
being and make me whole again.*

When my son Bill was seven years old, we were living in London. Although I did not know it, he had been saving his pocket money to buy me a gift. When the local bookshop had a going-out-of-business sale, he bought me a copy of *God's Psychiatry* by Dr. Charles L. Allen. Bill's eyes were wide with pride as he handed me my gift.

"I can't understand the "psy…" word, Mother, but I know you'd like to read about God," my son said.

I was very moved by his generous gift. Not only did I love my book, I have it to this day, underlined and treasured. I shall always be grateful to my son for introducing me to the writings of Charles Allen. His sensitive, compassionate books have been a source of joy to so many.

In *God's Psychiatry*, Dr. Allen tells of a man who came to him seeking help. He was greatly disturbed and longed for peace of mind. The "prescription" that Dr. Allen gave this man was a simple one, yet a very powerful one. He told him to read the Twenty-third Psalm five times a day, for seven days: reading it slowly and drinking in as much of the meaning as possible. Dr. Allen promised that at the end of the week he would have strengths he had never known before. He would feel healed. Needless to say, the prescription worked.

The Lord is my shepherd; I shall not want.
He maketh me to lie down in green pastures: he leadeth
me beside the still waters.
He restoreth my soul: he leadeth me in the paths of
righteousness for his name's sake.
Yea, though I walk through the valley of the shadow
of death, I will fear no evil: for thou art with me;
thy rod and thy staff they comfort me.
Thou preparest a table before me in the presence of
mine enemies: thou anointest my head with oil; my
cup runneth over.
Surely goodness and mercy shall follow me all the days
of my life: and I will dwell in the house of the Lord
for ever.

Whenever I need to restore peace of mind, I read the Twenty-third Psalm. If I am on my own, I read it aloud, emphasizing each word, stopping to absorb the glorious meaning. Afterwards, I always feel refreshed and comforted.

In the last letter I received from my father before he died, he wrote, "Each night before I go to sleep, I read the Twenty-third Psalm…" I know that he is with the Good Shepherd, forever.

In the early 1800's, T. B. Aldrich wrote a poem, entitled "Invocation to Sleep." It tells of the gift of sleep that God has given all creatures:

> *There is rest for all things. On still nights*
> *There is a folding of a million wings—*
> *The swarming honey-bees in unknown woods,*
> *The speckled butterflies and downy broods*
> *In dizzy poplar heights:*
> *Rest for innumerable nameless things,*
> *Rest for the creatures underneath the Sea,*
> *And in the Earth, and in the starry Air.…*

And even the lily of the field, the anemone, closes its petals at night, and not until sunrise does it once more start to unfold.

On troubled nights, when sleep seems to evade you, and you feel as if there can be no peace for you, remember that Jesus Christ, the Good Shepherd, is with you. Reach out for His hand in the darkness, and let His presence give you rest.

Thou hast touched me, and I have been
translated into thy peace.

Saint Augustine

Flax

joy

Flax flowers are a reflection of the sky above. The flower's bright face is made up of five blue petals with delicate violet markings at the base. It is a striking example of all the beauty that God has created. Although it is a dainty-looking plant, flax can grow to as tall as 36 inches. Its appearance belies its strength, because within the stems are the fibers used to make linen. In Biblical times, linen fibers were obtained by soaking the stems in water for several weeks. Long soaking made the linen fibers easy to separate. After being dried and bleached in the sun, the fibers were spun into linen thread and, then, woven into cloth. Flax seeds are the source of linseed oil.

Flax was growing long before the children of Israel arrived in Canaan. Moses referred to the fine linen that was made from the plant. We know it was used to make the sacred curtains for the court of the Tabernacle…"Thou shalt make the tabernacle with ten curtains of fine-twined linen…"

When Mary tenderly wrapped Jesus in swaddling clothes after His birth, it is believed that they were made of linen. And, when the disciples and Joseph of Arimathea prepared Jesus' body for burial, He was wrapped in linen cloth.

When Mary knew that she would go to Bethlehem with Joseph, she may have packed swaddling clothes for her coming baby and carried them on the donkey. Or, perhaps the innkeeper's wife provided them.

I wonder who it was that spun the linen to make those swaddling clothes? That unknown woman may never have known that the result of her labor would be so blessed as to be wrapped around the baby Jesus. How wonderful to have been able to make something for Him!

There are always unknown people who do so much for others and are never given recognition by society. But our Lord knows their hearts, and their reward is a lasting one. Jesus said, "It is more blessed to give than receive."

He gave His life on the Cross for us that we might know eternal joy. The linen that was wrapped around His body at his burial—I wonder, again, who it was that spun that cloth? There must have been sorrow if she knew that the result of her work was used for such a sad occasion, and yet it was a privilege to have been able to serve Him in that last act of love.

But what joy there was to come! When our Lord appeared to His followers as the Risen Savior, sorrow was forgotten, and the hope of all their tomorrows would be that one day they would be reunited with Him, forever. He had told them before the Crucifixion:

*"Do not let your hearts be troubled.
Trust in God; trust also in
me. In my Father's house are many
rooms; if it were not so, I would have told
you. I am going there to prepare a place
for you. And if I go and prepare a place
for you, I will come back and take you to
be with me that you also may be where
I am."*

John 14: 1-3

I love these words of Jesus because all the hope of eternal life is wrapped in them, comforting us like swaddling clothes. His words are direct. He does not say, "Perhaps I will be able to find a place for you." He promises us that he will. "If it were not so, I would have told you," is a statement that leaves no room for doubt.

When I stood outside the city walls of Jerusalem, near the sealed up Golden Gate, I saw a brilliant patch of blue flax growing wild. They danced in the wind, as if in joyous anticipation of that day when the Golden Gate will be opened once more for Jesus Christ to make His triumphant return.

And on that day everything will be made beautiful.

Heaven in a
Wild Flower

The mustard flower, the anemone, the rose of Sharon and flax flower have special memories for me, but in truth I love all flowers from the stately rose to the pesky dandelion. Flowers play an important role in our lives. They help to express our feelings for each other. On the birth of a baby, bouquets and plants are sent to celebrate the new life. Subsequent birthdays find flowers continuing to commemorate that person's special day. Weddings, too, call for flowers to echo the joy of the day. At funerals, flowers' beauty help us to remember that partings are not forever and that we will be joined with our Lord someday.

At home, I keep a large glass bowl filled with *pot-pourri* made from the flowers that my husband, Bill, has given me over the years. Some of the petals are from beautiful long-stemmed roses that I received on anniversaries, Valentine's Days and other happy occasions. Along with the aristocratic rose petals are the more mundane—those from tightly-held nosegays of wild flowers clutched in the tiny hands of my children and grandchildren. I treasure this bowl for it is filled with memories of joy.

In all ranks of life the human heart yearns
for the beautiful; and the beautiful things
that God makes are His gifts to all alike.

Harriet Beecher Stowe

Evidence of God's presence is all around us, but often we are too busy to notice His gifts—that perfect sunset, a dew drop caught in a filmy web, a stately day lily growing beside a grimy railroad track—they are there for us. Quiet gifts that can speak to our hearts, assuring us that He is here.

Speak to Him, thou, for He hears, and Spirit with
Spirit can meet —
Closer is He than breathing, and nearer than hands
and feet.

Alfred, Lord Tennyson

I love to visit the stately homes of England—grand estates that have become museums. They tell the story of life in an age of great fortunes. They show what these fortunes could buy—priceless art, ornate furnishing and armies of servants to keep them dusted.

As much as I delight in walking through these historic houses, it is the joy of being able to roam the magnificent grounds that I like the most.

There I can see trees that were planted hundreds of years before, some by famous landscape artists. Towering trees that have flourished through peace and war and are silent witnesses to God's faithfulness. I can see all the beauty He has created when I walk along worn paths where generations past once walked. At times like these, I thank Him for the beauty that He has given us.

Though I do not live in a stately home, from my window I can see many towering trees. Perhaps not as magnificent as those trimmed, fed and cosseted ones, but still miraculous. I can watch their never-ending cycle which speaks to me of the presence of an almighty and sovereign Creator. I am grateful for the quiet inner joy this knowledge brings.

For I have learned
To look on nature, not as in the hour
Of thoughtless youth, but hearing oftentimes
The still, sad music of humanity,
Nor harsh nor grating, though of ample power
To chasten and subdue. And I have felt
A presence that disturbs me with the joy
Of elevated thoughts; a sense sublime
Of something far more deeply interfused,
Whose dwelling is the light of setting suns,
And the round ocean, and the living air,
And the blue sky, and in the mind of man;
A motion and a spirit, that impels
All thinking things, all objects of all thought,
And rolls through all things.

William Wordsworth

Those of us who have the gift of sight too often miss the beauty that surrounds us. Sometimes it takes a special person to make us realize all that we have.

Helen Keller not only triumphed over blindness, but also over deafness and lack of speech. In an essay written by this remarkable woman entitled "Three Days to See", she told of what she would do if she was given the gift of sight for three days. She wrote of going to a great museum and being able to see the great Roman sculptures, instead of only being able to run her hands over their faces. She said that she would crowd in as much as possible in the short, joyous time given to her.

Frazier Hunt, a friend of Helen Keller, tells of a July afternoon in the Canadian Rockies when he watched her walk along a wagon trail, guided by a wire he had stretched along it for her. She stepped out into the sunlight and bent down to gather a handful of wolf willows, smelling their fragrance. She smiled, and her sightless eyes looked up into the sunlight. He heard her whisper, "Beautiful."

When I feel discouraged, or when events don't seem fair, or a pesky headache makes movement difficult, I often remember Helen Keller and that one word, "Beautiful." I tell myself, "Don't miss the joy that is all around you; and most important of all, the joy of Jesus Christ's presence within you…"

…surely I will be with you always…
Matthew 28:20

Have you ever watched people at an airport when a plane has just landed? I love to see the joyous anticipation as the people wait for loved ones coming through the barrier. A mother's expression lights up as she sees her daughter carrying a baby—she is about to meet her grandchild for the first time. A man stands anxiously waiting and then in a moment of joy is reunited with his wife. A couple peers through the crowd and sees their prodigal son returning to them. At first there is a moment's hesitancy when they see him, and then a healing smile breaks out and they all hug. They are wonderfully reunited.

Several years ago, after a long, bumpy, rather frightening flight to West Berlin, I walked off the plane, feeling very much a stranger in a strange land. Then in the distance I saw my husband waiting for me—a bouquet of flowers in his hands. What joy to see him standing there. I was not alone any longer.

Isn't this feeling a little like the joy we will experience when we finally get to heaven. We will be reunited with loved ones, in Jesus Christ, who has prepared a place for us there. Imagine what joy will be ours when we see Him for the first time, face to face!

Until then, there is much to be done in this world to let others know the beauty of His joy and love.

To see the World in a Grain of Sand
And a Heaven in a Wild Flower,
Hold Infinity in the palm of your hand
And Eternity in an hour.

William Blake